HALEAKALA
NATIONAL PARK

by Ruth Radlauer

Photographs
by Ed and Ruth Radlauer

Design and map
by Rolf Zillmer

AN ELK GROVE BOOK

 CHILDRENS PRESS®
CHICAGO

Each national park is a BEQUEST OF BEAUTY, a gift for those who follow. It is a place of special interest or beauty that has been set aside by the United States Government especially for you, your children, and their great-great-grandchildren. This bequest is yours to have and to care for so that others who follow can do the same during their lives.

To all those at Haleakala who helped.

Photo credits: Paul Banko, page 25 ('apapane) Haleakala National Park, Cover and pages 17 (top), 25 ('ua'u), 27 (nene) by R. C. Zink, 25 ('ua'u), 31 (goats) by Jim Larson, 35 Hawai'i Natural History Association, page 13 by Bob Seibert
U.S. Geological Survey, J. D. Griggs, page 47

Cover: Haleakala—House Of The Sun

Library of Congress Cataloging in Publication Data

Radlauer, Ruth Shaw.
    Haleakala National Park.
    (Parks for people)
    "An Elk Grove book."
    SUMMARY: Describes the delights to be found in the national park on the island of Maui in Hawaii.
    1.   Haleakala National Park—Juvenile literature.
[1.   Haleakala National Park.   2.   National parks and reserves.   3.   Hawaii—Description and travel]
I.   Radlauer, Edward.   II.   Zillmer, Rolf.   III.   Title.
DU628.H25R3   1979   919.69'21   79-10500
ISBN 0-516-07499-7

5 6 7 8 9 10 11 12 13 14 15 R 92 91 90 89 88 87

Contents

What is Haleakala National Park?

For ages of time it was a land of lava where cloudy mists watered plants found only in Hawai'i. For thousands of years it has been one of the two natural homes of the rarest goose in the world, the nene. Hundreds of years ago, Hawaiians named it Haleakala, "house of the sun."

Today people gaze from the rim of this mountaintop valley, incorrectly named a crater. Sometimes the valley's depth is hidden in clouds. But patient visitors wait while the "curtain rises," and "house of the sun" comes into view.

Haleakala National Park is hiking in sun or in rain. It's camping at Hosmer Grove or by the ocean at 'Ohe'o. For some, it's an overnight horse ride to Paliku.

This park is also the green valleys of 'Ohe'o Gulch where rushing streams flow into the sea.

Which will be your Haleakala? The one you see from the crater's rim? The one you ride through on a horse? Or will it be the one that scrunches under your feet when you are a tiny dot in the bottom of the crater?

page 4

Native Bunch Grass—Deschampsia

Nene—Wild Hawaiian Goose

Sliding Sands Trail

'Ohe'o

Where is Haleakala National Park?

Haleakala National Park is on the eastern part of Maui, one of the islands that make up the state of Hawai'i.

To get there from the mainland, you take a plane to Honolulu on the island of O'ahu. Another plane takes you to Kahului, Maui. Sometimes you can take a plane directly to Maui without going first to Honolulu.

In a rented car or a tour bus, you travel on Highways 37, 377, and 378 to the crater. A short distance from the entrance is Park Headquarters where you can get a map, ask questions, and buy books and post cards.

At the top of Haleakala is the Visitor Center. Here you can see most of the crater when it's clear. In the Visitor Center, a park ranger explains how the crater formed and tells who and what lives there.

Another part of this park is near the coast in the Kipahulu District. It's reached on a slow, winding road, Highway 36. At the town of Hana, you take Highway 31 to 'Ohe'o.

For a map and information about camping, write to the Superintendent, Haleakala National Park, P. O. Box 369, Makawao, Maui, Hawai'i 96768.

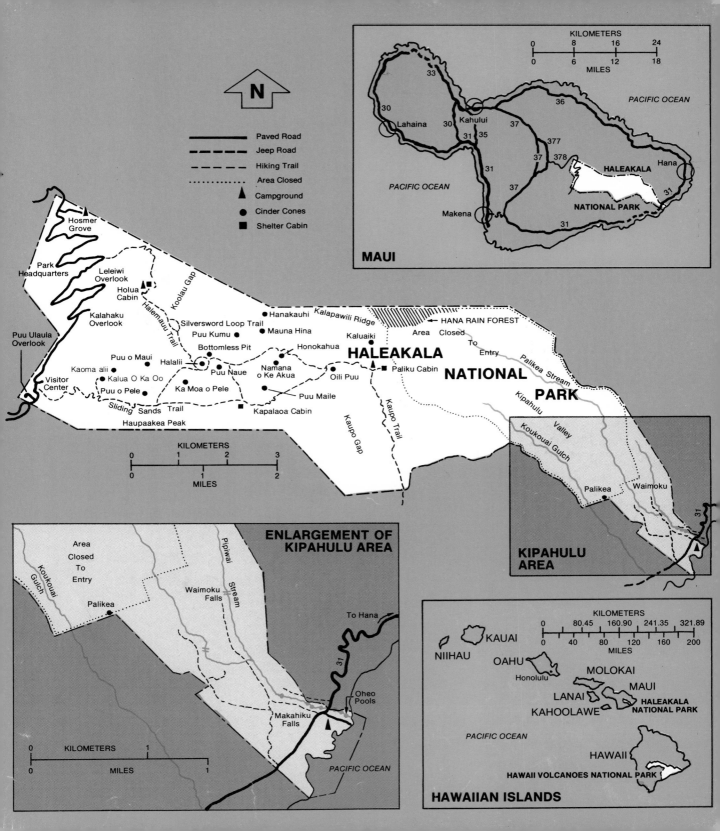

Legend
- Paved Road
- Jeep Road
- Hiking Trail
- Area Closed
- ▲ Campground
- ● Cinder Cones
- ■ Shelter Cabin

MAUI

KILOMETERS
0 8 16 24
MILES
0 6 12 18

PACIFIC OCEAN

33
30
30 Kahului
Lahaina 31 35
36
37
377
378
37
31
HALEAKALA
Hana
37
31
NATIONAL PARK
Makena
31
PACIFIC OCEAN
31

HALEAKALA NATIONAL PARK

Hosmer Grove
Park Headquarters
Leleiwi Overlook
Holua Cabin
Koolau Gap
Kalahaku Overlook
Puu Ulaula Overlook
Halemauu Trail
Hanakauhi
Kalapawili Ridge
HANA RAIN FOREST
Area Closed
Silversword Loop Trail
Mauna Hina
Puu Kumu
Kaluaiki
To Entry
Palikea Stream
Bottomless Pit
Honokahua
Puu o Maui
Halalii
Puu Naue
Namana o Ke Akua
Oili Puu
Paliku Cabin
Kaoma alii
Kalua O Ka Oo
Puu o Pele
Ka Moa o Pele
Puu Maile
Kipahulu Valley
Visitor Center
Sliding Sands Trail
Kapalaoa Cabin
Kaupo Gap
Kaupo Trail
Koukouai Gulch
Haupaakea Peak
Palikea
Waimoku

KILOMETERS
0 1 2 3
MILES
0 1 2

KIPAHULU AREA

31

ENLARGEMENT OF KIPAHULU AREA

Koukouai Gulch
Area Closed To Entry
Palikea
Pipiwai Stream
Waimoku Falls
To Hana
31
Makahiku Falls
Oheo Pools
PACIFIC OCEAN

KILOMETERS
0 1
MILES
0 1

HAWAIIAN ISLANDS

KILOMETERS
0 80.45 160.90 241.35 321.89
MILES
0 40 80 120 160 200

NIIHAU
KAUAI
OAHU
Honolulu
MOLOKAI
LANAI
MAUI
KAHOOLAWE
HALEAKALA NATIONAL PARK
PACIFIC OCEAN
HAWAII
HAWAII VOLCANOES NATIONAL PARK

How to "Speak Hawaiian"

At first you may find it hard to say all these Hawaiian words. But when written with the English alphabet, this beautiful language uses only 12 letters and a symbol ('). The consonants are *h, k, l, m, n, p,* and *w.* These all sound the same as they do in English except that "w" sounds as "v" when it comes after "e" or "i." At the beginning of a word or after "a," "w" can have a "v" or "w" sound. The glottal stop ('), or 'okina, is also considered a consonant.

The vowels are *a, e, i, o,* and *u,* and sound like this: a as in *saw* or *alone*; e as in *they*; i as in *machine*; o as in *no*; u as in *moon*.

When the vowels pile up together in a word like "Maui," you say, "Mah oo ee," and run it all together.

When a vowel is repeated, as in the word, *ali'i* and *pua'a*, you just say the sound twice: *ah lee ee* and *poo ah ah*. This symbol, ('), is called a glottal stop, or 'okina. Between two vowels in a word like *'ua'u*," it means a tiny voice pause, a glottal stop.

Here are some words you'll want to know when you visit Hawai'i.

A Few Hawaiian Words

'ahinahina silversword, native flowering plant found only on Maui and Hawai'i

'akala native Hawaiian raspberry

akua god

ali'i chief

aloha welcome, love, farewell, greetings

amakihi small yellow-green and black bird of the honeycreeper family

'ama'u (plural 'ama'uma'u) large fern native to Hawai'i

'apapane honeycreeper bird with red body and black wings

hale house

Haleakala house of the sun

Halemau'u grass hut; also trail on west wall of crater

Hana bay or valley when used in the name of a place

Haumea goddess, Pele's mother

heiau temple

Hina Maui's mother

Holua sled; also name of crater cabin

'i'iwi small bright red bird of honeycreeper family

kahuna priest

kane male

Kapalaoa whaletooth ivory pendant worn by royalty; also name of a cabin in crater

kapu forbidden act—taboo

kaulua double hulled canoe

Kaupo to land at night; native banana; name of village and of a gap in the crater

Kipahulu worn out soil or a place where soil has been worn out by farming; district of Haleakala National Park on east coast of Maui

Ko'olau windward side of Hawaiian Islands; name of gap in the crater

kukaenene low trailing shrub; favorite food of nene

Ku-waha-ilo Pele's father, a god who lived in the sky; Ku with the wormy mouth

lehua red blossoms of the 'ohi'a tree—See 'ohi'a.

Leleiwi carved figure on the bowsprit of a canoe or ship; name of cliff where Halemau'u Trail goes into crater

mahalo thank you

Makahiku waterfall in 'Ohe'o

makai toward the sea; opposite of mauka; See mauka.

Makawao district on slope of Haleakala

mamane also mamani; native tree or shrub with yellow flower

Maui demigod for whom one of the islands is named; a variety of sweet potato

mauka inland

mauna mountain

moa jungle fowl

Na-Maka (short for Na-Maka-o-Kaha'i) goddess of the sea, Pele's sister

nene Hawaiian goose, Hawai'i state bird, protected and very rare

'ohelo small native shrub often given to Pele in tribute

'Ohe'o gorge with many waterfalls and pools; a gulch in Kipahulu District of the park

'ohi'a native Hawaiian tree with red blossom—See lehua.

'ohi'a-lehua See 'ohi'a and lehua.

pa fence, wall, corral, pen, sty

pali cliff

Pele goddess of fire, volcano goddess

pua flower

pua'a pig

pu'u hill

pu'u ula'ula red hill

Pu'uloa long hill

'ua'u dark-rumped petrel; rare bird widespread in Eastern Pacific

Waimoku waterfall at top of 'Ohe'o

wahine female

wiki hurry

wikiwiki hurry very fast

How to "Speak Volcano"

The state of Hawaiʻi is made of lava, so you hear a lot about volcanoes when you visit the islands.

You may already know some volcano words: *lava, eruption, ash, cinder.* But some of the words are strange: *lapilli, ejecta, spatter.*

Many scientists come to Hawaiʻi to study volcanoes. They like to visit Haleakala and Hawaiʻi Volcanoes National Parks. Haleakala Volcano is thought to be *dormant,* or inactive, not *extinct.* And the volcanoes on the island of Hawaiʻi are very *active.* That's why some Hawaiian words have been added to the language of volcanoes: *aa, pahoehoe, Pele's hair, Pele's tears.*

Some of the volcano words on page 11 appear in this book. Others will help you understand what's going on when park people start to "speak volcano."

But you'd better watch out. In Hawaiʻi, you could catch a bad case of *volcanology* and turn into a *volcanologist.* What's volcanology? Look on page 11.

'a'a — rough, chunky lava

active volcano — volcano that still erupts

ash — fine-grained ejecta—See *ejecta*.

blocks — jagged ejecta over 2½ inches across

bombs — smooth, rounded ejecta over 2½ inches across

breccia — mass of jagged rock fragments banded together

caldera — very large volcanic crater formed by the collapse of the top of a volcano

cascade — lava flowing down a cliff or steep hill

cinder — spongy bits of lava the size of a pea or larger

cinder cone — cone-shaped hill of cinder piled up around a vent

conduits — passageways inside a volcano

crater — basin or bowl around the vent of a volcano formed by explosion or collapse of volcano top

dormant volcano — fairly active volcano in its quiet period

ejecta — volcanic fragments thrown out, or ejected, by explosion

erosional crater — basin cut out, or eroded, by water

erupt — to come out with force; in a volcano, to spout or throw out lava, gas, ash, etc.

extinct volcano — volcano not expected to erupt again

fault — break, or fracture, in the earth's crust—Both sides of the fault have moved in relation to each other.

fumarole — hole from which gases come from inside the earth

hot spot — extra hot place in the earth's mantle with enough heat to melt rock—As the Pacific Plate moves over a hot spot under the Pacific Ocean, volcanoes erupt and create islands.

inactive — dormant or quiet

lapilli — ejecta from about ¾ to 2½ inches across—One is a *lapillus*.

lava — hot liquid rock at or close to earth's surface and its cooled, hardened products—See *magma*.

lava tube — natural tunnel in a lava flow caused by draining of the flow beneath a solid surface

magma — hot liquid rock; lava stored inside the earth

magma reservoirs — areas in the earth's crust where magma collects

pahoehoe — lava with a smooth or ropelike surface

Pele's hair — volcanic glass, spun out by wind to look like hair

Pele's tears — hardened lava droplets

pumice — lava full of air holes caused by gas escaping when the lava was molten

rift — fractured area in earth's crust

rift zone — highly fractured belt on the side, or flank, of a volcano where most eruptions take place

seismograph — instrument to measure movements in the earth's crust

shield volcano — domelike volcano, such as Kilauea and Mauna Loa, with gentle sloping sides

spatter — very liquid ejecta that flatten when they hit the ground—They often stick together.

spatter cone — pile of spatter built up into a cone shape

tremor — trembling of ground caused by movement of magma through volcanic passageways called conduits

tuff — volcanic ash that has welded together

vent — hole where lava comes out

volcano — break or hole in the earth where magma flows out as lava; also the mound, hill, or mountain created by eruption of lava

volcanologist — scientist who studies volcanoes

volcanology — study of volcanoes

What is a Volcano?

A volcano is a hole where melted rock called magma comes up from inside the earth. As soon as magma is above ground, it's lava. Volcano is also a word for the hill or mountain built by many eruptions of lava. But where do lava and magma come from?

About 20 miles under the surface, the earth is hot enough to melt rock. Under the earth's crust, rocks are usually under too much pressure to melt. But some rocks do melt. They become magma and collect in places called magma reservoirs. When magma gets hot enough and full of gases, it flows toward cracks or holes in the crust. The magma roars out of the hole as red hot lava.

The Hawaiian Islands were created when a piece of the earth's crust, the Pacific Plate, moved over a very hot spot in the earth's lower layer, the mantle. Over millions of years, the hot spot melted the crust in different places and created volcanoes.

Volcanoes in Hawai'i are not as dangerous as some in other parts of the world. The lava is very liquid with a low content of gas, so it erupts with less force. When a Hawaiian volcano erupts, people run to see it—but very carefully!

Mauna Loa Eruption At 9400′ Elevation—Hawai'i Volcanoes National Park

Maui— the Island

The island of Maui is made up of two huge volcanic mountains connected by a stretch of flat land. But for a very, very long time, the volcanoes that created Maui have been dormant, quiet, as if sleeping.

Each volcano began millions of years ago at the bottom of the Pacific Ocean. The lava cooled and lay in a mound. Every time the volcano erupted, it added a layer of lava to the mound. Countless times through countless years, the volcano erupted again and again until it grew high above the level of the sea. An island had been born.

In this way, a long chain of islands formed in the Pacific Ocean. The last 132 islands of this chain make up the state of Hawai'i.

Most Hawaiians live on seven of the eight main islands which are named Ni'ihau, Kaua'i, O'ahu, Moloka'i, Lana'i, Kaho'olawe, Maui, and Hawai'i. Maui and Hawai'i were the last to form between one and three millions years ago.

Island of Maui Seen From Haleakala ▶

Craters

A *crater* is like a bowl around the vent, or hole, where a volcano erupts. Some craters are formed by explosion. Others form when the top of the volcano sinks or collapses.

When a crater gets very wide, it is called a *caldera*. Sometimes a volcano erupts and makes a crater within its caldera.

Scientists believe that Haleakala Volcano once reached an elevation of 12,000 feet above the sea. But even as a volcano grows, it brings about its own destruction. As air currents or wind move across the ocean, they pick up water vapor. When air currents meet the volcanic mountain, they rise. The water vapor cools and turns into mist, then into raindrops.

Heavy rainfall eroded the heights of Haleakala. Two deep valleys formed and joined to make a huge basin. After thousands of years of erosion, Haleakala erupted some more and filled the valleys with lava flows and cinder cones.

So you see, the "crater" at Haleakala is not a true crater. It's a mountaintop depression, also called an *erosional crater*.

Haleakala—An Erosional Crater Seen From Hana Kauhi

A Crater Within A Caldera—Hawai'i Volcanoes National Park

Life Begins

Imagine these lush green islands without a sign of life: no grass, no trees, no animals, just lava. How could life begin?

The first life to cling to the islands was a blue-green alga that came from the sea. Lichens may have come next. A lichen is a combination of an alga and a fungus, which is like mold. As lichen grows on rocks, it helps break them into bits that later become part of the soil.

Later, winds carried spores from distant lands to the islands. Drawing life from algae-covered lava, the spores grew into ferns and mosses. These plants died and decayed. Then, as tiny bits of lava washed down from the hills, they mixed with decayed plants and formed soil. But what grew in the soil? For a while, there were just more spores to make more mosses and ferns.

Even today in the crater, this same succession of plants goes on. You'll find ferns of all sizes tucked in among the lava. They grow, die, and mix with lava bits to make soil where seeds can sprout. But how did seeds get to these islands in the middle of the Pacific Ocean?

Kupukupu Fern—Ferns, Mosses, And Lichens Came First

'Ama'uma'u Fern—Halemau'u Trail

Flowering Plants

Seeds come from flowering plants like 'akala, 'ohi'a, and mamane. But how did the first seeds get to Hawai'i?

Floating on water, sailing on wind, or caught among bird feathers, seeds finally reached the islands. In warm sun and constant rain, the seeds sank their roots into the rich lava soil.

For thousands of years, native Hawaiian plants evolved, or developed. Separated from the mainland, they evolved without predators to hurt them. With no large mammals to eat or trample them, these native plants gave up protective things like thorns and bitter poisons.

But finally predators did come. Pigs came in canoes with early Hawaiians. Goats landed with some of the explorers. Early settlers brought mainland plants that escaped from backyard gardens and grew wild.

A few years ago, the evening primrose landed in the crater. Now it has almost covered the crater floor.

No one can send back all the plants and animals people have brought here. But the Park Service is working to make Haleakala more like it was before people came to Hawai'i.

'Akala—Native Hawaiian Raspberry

Mamane—Native Hawaiian

Non-Native Evening Primrose

Silversword

In Haleakala you will see one of the rarest plants in the world, the silversword. This plant looks something like the yucca. But it belongs to the same family as the sunflower, the composite family.

The swordlike leaves of this plant are covered with tiny silver hairs. These hairs reflect sunlight and keep the plant from drying out.

The 'ahinahina, as Hawaiians call it, grows for 4 to 20 years. When the plant is big and strong, the center begins to grow taller until it's about three feet high. Then the center stalk blooms with hundreds of small blossoms that later go to seed. After blooming only once, the silversword dies.

When you see this plant, you must take care not to kill it. Silversword grows in cinder, which is razor sharp. If you walk too close, the cinder shifts and cuts the shallow roots.

You can see this Hawaiian beauty in an enclosure on the road below the Visitor Center. Silverswords also grow here and there in the crater, especially on the Silversword Loop Trail.

Silversword In Bloom

Tiny Hairs Reflect Sunlight

Birds

In a distant time, thousands of years ago, some birds found Hawai'i. Among them was one species, or kind, of honeycreeper. Over a very long time, this bird changed, or evolved, into more than 20 different species of honeycreepers. Each species evolved a different shaped bill to eat different foods. The red 'i'iwi's bill is curved so it can reach into lobelia and other deep flowers. The 'apapane's bill is long enough to reach into the red pompom flowers of the 'ohi'a-lehua tree and the throat of yellow mamane flowers.

A vanishing bird species still nests in the crater from March to October. During the breeding season, the 'ua'u, or dark-rumped petrel, makes a nest in the highest cliffs of the crater walls. The 'ua'u spends its days out over the ocean, probably feeding on sea life. At night it returns to the crater.

Hikers often hear a doglike yap that seems to circle in the dark sky. It's the 'ua'u, returning to its nest after a day at sea.

The 'ua'u is in danger, because it lays only one egg a year. It is also in danger from predators such as rats and wild, or feral, cats.

'Apapane—Native Hawaiian Honeycreeper

'Ua'u—Dark-Rumped Petrel

The best places in Haleakala to see birds are Hosmer Grove and Paliku. In the crater at Paliku, you will probably see the nene, the very rare Hawaiian Goose. Some believe the nene evolved from a Canadian goose that flew off course thousands of years ago. Now the nene has evolved into a separate species. With almost no fresh water in which to swim, its webbed feet have changed from water-paddlers to lava-walkers.

From October to May, the nene nests high in the mountains. A mother lays two to eight eggs. But many of the eggs and goslings get eaten by mongooses. The average mother nene raises only one gosling a year.

When the goslings can fly, the geese come down from the heights. Near Paliku, they feed on berries and hairy cat's ear, which looks like dandelion.

While you may see this endangered bird in a zoo, it is found naturally only on Maui and Hawai'i. State game and park officials raise nene in pens. Later the geese are released in the two Hawaiian national parks where they have a chance to survive and increase in numbers.

Nene

Nene

Hairy Cat's Ear—A Favorite With Nene

Nene Food—Kukae-nene

Early People

As early as A. D. 800, Haleakala was a sacred, or holy place to Hawaiians. From the western slope, people brought their dead here to bury them. From the Kaupo area they came to perform ceremonies for their babies.

Some places in the crater were so sacred that a person who disturbed the sand "might die."

Hawaiians built altars and temples in the crater. They also chipped out hunks of hard lava rocks for making tools. People used crater trails to cross Maui instead of going through dense forests around the base of the mountain.

From a rock above Paliku, early Hawaiians marked straight lines all the way to the sea on the east. In this way, they marked the boundaries for pie-shaped divisions of land which were ruled by chiefs, or *ali'i.* The *kahuna,* or priests, told the main ali'i how the gods wanted him to rule the people.

If you see the remains of stone altars or houses, leave them alone for others to see. Besides, scientists are still studying these rocks to find out more about the first people who came to Haleakala.

An Akua—Hawaiian God—Bishop Museum

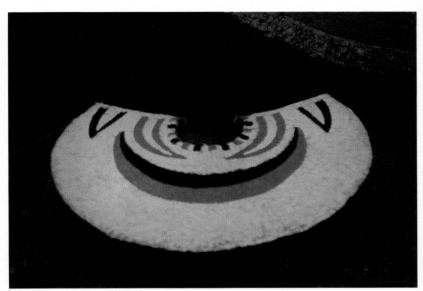

Feather Cape Worn by Ali'i—Bishop Museum, Honolulu

East Maui Was Cut Off By Dense Forests—'Ohe'o

Exotics — Animals Out of Place

For a food supply, the Hawaiians brought plants and animals to the islands. But insects and rodents, such as rats and mice, also made the journey, hidden in the cargo.

Many years later, European explorers imported goats to give milk and provide meat. Other people introduced deer, pheasants, and chukars for game hunting.

Later, the mongoose was introduced to catch rats in the sugar cane fields. But it didn't work because a mongoose hunts by day and rats work at night.

All of these animals, called *exotics,* are out of place. They upset the natural balance that Hawai'i had before people came. Some goats became wild, or feral. Now they graze on valuable grasses and destroy mamane bushes. Worst of all, goats endanger the silversword by eating the growing heart of the plant. Wild pigs root among ferns and kill them. The mongoose eats the eggs and young of the 'ua'u and nene.

The National Park Service has a program to get rid of exotics. If it works, Haleakala will be more like it was in the beginning.

Exotics—Feral Goats

Chukar—Also Exotic

The Legends of Maui

Hawaiian legends tell about Maui, a demigod who was full of tricks. He taught people to make fire by rubbing sticks together. He made birds visible so people could see as well as hear them. And Maui invented spears and barbed fishhooks. He even fashioned a giant fishhook from his dead grandmother's jawbone. With it he fished the Hawaiian Islands up from the bottom of the sea.

The islands were covered with darkness and clouds until Maui pushed the heavens far above the highest mountains. But even now, when Maui sleeps, the heavens creep back down and cover the islands with storms.

The island women said there wasn't enough sunlight to dry the cloth they made from bark. So Maui wove some rope with his sister's hair and attached it to the giant jawbone fishhook. From high on the mountain, he threw his hook and caught the sun by its rays. The sun struggled and pleaded, ''Give me my life!''

After a while, Maui let go. But first he made the sun promise to go more slowly as it passed over Maui's home. And to this day they call the mountain Haleakala, house of the sun.

Demigod Maui

The Legends of Pele

Some legends say that Pele gave fire to Maui before Maui gave it to the world. Pele was the volcano goddess of fire. One version of her story says her mother was Haumea, and Ku-waha-ilo, or "Ku with the wormy mouth," was her father.

Pele's favorite brother was king of the sharks. Her worst enemy was an older sister, a sea goddess named Na-maka-o-kahai. Because water puts out fire, Pele tried to get away from Na-maka. Beginning in the northwest, Pele dug a crater on each of the islands, trying to hide from Na-maka's weapons, waves, rain, and floods. But Na-maka overwhelmed each volcano and threatened to put out Pele's fire.

Pele fled from Ni'ihau to Kaua'i, then to O'ahu and the other islands. On each island she built a new crater, only to have it worn down by waves and rain. Finally, the sea goddess even chased Pele away from the island of Maui.

According to legend, Pele is now living in Kilauea Volcano on the island of Hawai'i. If Na-maka finds her there, Pele may have to build another volcano beyond the newest of the Hawaiian Islands.

Legend Says Pele Once Lived Here—Kaoma-aliʻi Cinder Cone

To Know this Crater

You can go into the crater on a horse or on foot. You may go just a little way or all the way across. Most people who go in on the Sliding Sands Trail go out at a lower elevation. This trail starts at an elevation above 9700 feet where you get less oxygen with every breath.

To use the cabins in the crater, you must write to the park at least three months in advance. Each of the three cabins has running water, outdoor toilets, wood stoves and wood, and padded bunks.

Otherwise you can get a permit to camp near Paliku or Holua cabins. Open fires are not allowed, so campers need backpack stoves.

Any way you choose to go into the crater, you need to carry water on the trail. And be prepared for hot sun, cold weather, or rain. These can all happen in one day.

Once in the crater, you will know a silence that may surprise you. In the silence you will hear goats, chukars, and maybe even nene. And at night, you'll see more stars than you have ever seen before.

Be Prepared For Rain

Halemau'u Trail—Leleiwi Pali (Cliff)

Feel Small In The Crater

Pele's Lava

Legends say that Pele caused the lava flows you see from the crater rim. If you hike in the crater, you see that the flows are made up mostly of a chunky kind of lava called *aa.*

The smoother lava, that looks like icing on a cake, is *pahoehoe.* During an eruption, pahoehoe sometimes hardens and forms a crust on the surface. The lava underneath stays red-hot and flows along under this crust. When the flow stops, there is often an empty tube or tunnel left in the lava. If you have a good flashlight and caving gear, you can ask a park official about exploring a lava tube.

At times a volcano throws out blobs of lava that cool and harden before they hit the earth. Blobs bigger than baseballs are called *bombs.* If lava is still soft when it hits the ground, it spatters. You'll see many globs of spatter in the crater. Sometimes tubes and holes in the spatter show where gas escaped as the lava cooled.

Pea-sized bits of lava full of bubbles make up the cinder of Haleakala's famous cinder cones.

Lava Tube

Spatter

Pele's Crater

Pele, goddess of fire, made many other strange lava shapes that dot the crater floor. As you follow the trail over lava flows, you see weird piles of aa that look like tortured beasts from the past.

Peering into the Bottomless Pit, you see a vent where superheated gases once belched forth during an eruption. Was the rim around it colored by gas and heat or by Pele's paintbrush?

When lava is very liquid, it spatters into the air and falls in a pile called a *spatter cone*. Pa puaʻa o Pele, Pele's Pig Pen, is the rim of a spatter cone, now partly buried in cinder.

And speaking of Pele, you must be careful not to "borrow" any of her lava. It's against park regulations, and many believe Pele sends bad luck along with any lava that visitors carry home. Almost daily, little packages arrive at Park Headquarters. A letter in each package usually says something like, "I'm sorry, Pele. I'm returning your lava along with all my bad luck (I hope)."

Spatter Cone Rim Named Pele's Pig Pen

Pele's Lava

'Ohe'o

'Ohe'o is a gorge with many waterfalls and pools. To see 'Ohe'o in the Kipahulu District of the park, you must travel three or four hours on a narrow, winding road.

Streams fed by heavy rainfall cut 'Ohe'o and the Kipahulu Valley. The water tumbles down steep lava pali, or cliffs, in graceful white waterfalls. At the base of these falls are chilly, clear plunge pools.

People settled here as early as A.D. 750. Great numbers of them farmed and fished in this coastal paradise. The dense rain forest cut them off from the wars that raged between other groups on the rest of Maui.

Plan to walk if you visit 'Ohe'o. You'll be winding your way around the gorge on paths once traveled by early Hawaiians. The Makai, or seaward, Trail takes you along the lower pools. The Mauka, or inland, Trail leads to a view of Makahiku Falls. With time and energy, you can follow the trail farther up to Waimoku Falls at the head of the gorge known as 'Ohe'o.

Makahiku Falls—'Ohe'o ▶

A Very Special Place

Hawai'i is a very special place. You might even call it "Mother Nature's Experimental Laboratory." Here on these islands far from large land masses, new life forms developed. But it took thousands of years while no predators interfered with the "experiments."

Most of the native flowering plants and two-thirds of the ferns are found *only* in Hawai'i. Some of the birds and lava tube life are just as special.

But ever since A.D. 750, people have been coming to Hawai'i. In a short time, they have introduced thousands of non-native plants and animals.

Predators eat or damage many of the native species. Introduced plants like ginger, non-native orchids, and garden flowers often go wild, take over, and crowd out native plants. Non-native birds have brought diseases that kill Hawai'i's rare birds.

But there are two national parks in Hawai'i where "Mother Nature's Laboratory" is protected. So walk softly in these very special places. Take care of the "experiments" in Haleakala National Park.

An Experiment?—'Ama'uma'u Fern Uncurls ▶

Another National Park in Hawai'i

On the Big Island is HAWAI'I VOLCANOES NATIONAL PARK. It's a changing place where active volcanoes still erupt.

Guided activities in this park include nature talks and volcano movies at the Visitor Center. Self-guiding nature walks on Sandalwood or Bird Park Trails give visitors a look at native plants and birds.

On a short walk through a fern forest, visitors find themselves in a lava tube. Long and short hikes go along or around the edge of Kilauea Volcano's caldera. More difficult trails cross Kilauea's two craters within the caldera.

Backpackers will find cabins and shelters for overnight hikes available on a first come, first served basis. They go up Mauna loa or other remote parts of the park.

Write to the Superintendent, Hawai'i Volcanoes National Park, Box 52, Hawai'i National Park, HI, 96718, for information about cabins, campgrounds, and the hotel.

The Author and Illustrators

Wyoming-born Ruth Radlauer's love affair with national parks began in Yellowstone. During her younger years, she spent her summers in the Bighorn Mountains, in Yellowstone, or on Casper Mountain.

Ed and Ruth Radlauer, graduates of the University of California at Los Angeles, are authors of many books for young people. Along with their adult daughter and sons, they photograph and write about a wide variety of subjects ranging from monkeys to motorcycles.

The Radlauers live in California, where Ruth and Ed spend most of their time in the mountains near Los Angeles.

*　　*　　*

Ruth and Ed are especially grateful to Carl J. Leibel, who published their first books.